Tales

THE ART OF
CHRISTIAN ALZMANN

designstudio|PRESS

Tales, the Art of Christian Alzmann

Contact: www.christianalzmann.com

Copyright © 2013 Design Studio Press
All Rights Reserved.

All text and artwork in this book are copyright © 2013 Christian Alzmann. No parts of this book may be reproduced or transmitted in any form or by any means, electronic or mechanical, including photocopying, xerography, and videography recording without written permission from the publisher, Design Studio Press.

Copy Editor: Anne Fisher Gonzales, Jessica Hoffmann
Book Design: Christian Alzmann, Cecilia Zo

Published by Design Studio Press
8577 Higuera Street
Culver City, CA 90232
Website: www.designstudiopress.com
E-mail: info@designstudiopress.com

Printed in China
First Edition, July 2013

10 9 8 7 6 5 4 3 2 1

Library Of Congress Control Number: 2013935810

ISBN-13: 978-1624650-00-0

Table of Contents

FOREWORD 7
INTRODUCTION 8
SKETCHES 10
PAINTINGS 35
TUTORIAL 94
AFTERWORD 103
SPECIAL THANKS 104

Dedication

To all of the great teachers and people who have inspired me through the years and, most importantly, to my wife, Andrea. Without her, what follows would never have made it to print.

Foreword

by Aaron McBride

I occupy an ironic position in Christian Alzmann's career. You see, I stole his job.

We were both considered for a position in the art department at Industrial Light & Magic in 1999, and, purely on a fluke of timing, I landed the job. Another spot opened up shortly, and Christian came on board. But I technically had two months' seniority on him, a point that became increasingly embarrassing for me over the next year, as it became painfully evident that Christian was infinitely more artistically gifted than I was.

We were all a bit envious of him when he started. He was sort of a savant when it came to painting. Light and color just made sense to him. As production assistant, his job was supposed to be ordering office supplies and making photocopies. But within a week he became one of the most sought-after artists in the department. He was initially tasked with helping to design the first digital feature in ILM's burgeoning Animated Features Division. Soon, art directors and commercial directors were constantly clamoring for him to design and paint shot concepts to render them more cinematic. And he did it in the same way that anyone with an extraordinary and prodigious talent does. He made it look easy.

Soon after, Christian and I were assigned to be concept artists on Steven Spielberg's A.I. Artificial Intelligence.

Christian crafted the palette for the underwater amusement park within a few hours. In an effort to keep pace with the richness with which he was bringing this watery world to cinematic life, I was forced to stay late at work, sampling colors from his paintings, pixel by pixel, in Photoshop. I attempted to emulate the vibrant tapestry illuminated by his effortless mixing of colors. It was a tedious and time-consuming process, but still probably faster and less daunting than trying to match painting skills with him.

Christian's great strength is consistently striking that balance between what's aesthetically attractive and what's real. Often an artist may err too far towards the pretty, and an illustration can be overly sentimental or quaint. Striving for strict realism can turn a painting cold, terse, and alienating. Christian's forte is playing the romantic qualities of light off its hard truths, counter-weighing stunningly lyric forms with their ferociously wicked complements.

Like a fragile accord delicately reached, a painting that may at first seem innocent and playful in its palette draws you in and you are suddenly confronted with quite ominous and terrifying forms staring back at you. My favorite works of Christian's are the ones where that icy chill is a second read. Like staring out a window at night and seeing your reflection, and then realizing the kid from Salem's Lot is staring back through the window at you.

These moments he captures may have never existed. But the depictions resonate with viewers, like watching a favorite film from childhood. Or the comic book you read and re-read until it was dog-eared.

Each painting, illustration, and sketch is a tale you want to follow, descending deeper into his world. Every brush stroke, every shadow, value, or cross-hatch is a precious piece of a complex narrative. Your eyes move feverishly from one figure or silhouette to the next, like a reader of an epic novel, savoring a page before eagerly turning to the next.

Christian's work and the moments, stories, and characters portrayed continue to be the images of pure uncompromised imagination. To say that his work has been an indelible source of inspiration to me would be a vast understatement.

And so, 15 years after I stole his job, the artist, his talent, and his art still show me how to tell my own authentic tale.

Introduction

One of the first things I remember drawing…

I guess a lot of art books start out this way, so in the grand tradition I'll just continue. One of the first things I remember drawing is Darth Vader in finger paint during crafts time in kindergarten. I distinctly remember some of the other students gathering around after saying that they thought it looked like Darth Vader. Since I painted it from memory and everyone liked it, I guess that helped give me an itch to do more. Well, that and really supportive parents.

Growing up in the 1970s and '80s, it was really difficult to find imagery from your favorite movies. There wasn't even VHS tape at that point, so if I wanted to see those amazing film images again I had to learn to draw them. Star Wars started it and many other films and books followed.

By the time I was in high school Disney was starting to make a solid comeback with movies like The Little Mermaid. Needless to say, the whole Disney collection was very inspiring to me, so I alternated between looking at matte paintings and concepts from ILM and making animated flip books out of tracing-paper pads all through high school. In my junior year a friend and I had heard about CalArts, a famed art school about 40 minutes away from where we lived. They were known for training animators that get hired by Disney right out of school. We took the tour and I remember being totally nuts about the whole place. At the end of the tour our guide gave everyone a current catalog. We looked at it as we walked around, and lo and behold in the back were the tuition and housing costs. Art schools are expensive, so my dreams were crushed, at least for a while. I put it out of my mind and went to community college to see what else was out there for me.

After too many enjoyable years studying everything that interested me at community college, I realized I was in danger of going nowhere. So I asked myself the question that took me years of junior college to find: what is it that you want to do for 40 hours a week, week in, week out? There was only one real answer: draw. I just wanted to draw and make images. With the support of my then girlfriend, now wife, I filled out an application to The Art Center in Pasadena. By this point I was leaning more towards illustration and wanted to go to the same school that Ralph McQuarrie and Syd Mead went to because I realized that what fascinated me about pictures is the stories that they tell, the visual theater of it. That was the common link to everything I loved.

I put a portfolio together and got accepted. This was one of the happiest moments I can remember having. I was on my way to becoming an artist.

There were great classes there and great teachers and, of course, some really difficult financial times too. I learned to paint figures in oils and to draw in perspective. I also learned to learn more on my own, which was the most valuable thing art school taught me. My last term at Art Center we had the option of signing up for on-campus interviews.

To my amazement Industrial Light & Magic was one of the companies on the list. I of course knew of all of their work and had heard of many of their employees through "making of" shows, books, and magazines.
I was a bit worried going into the interview, because at the time I had two portfolios to show, neither of which was a live-action film portfolio, which is what I thought they would want to see. The one I brought was geared towards visual development for feature animation.

I figured ILM would not be interested, but I had to give it a try. At the very least, I would get to meet some of the talented people from ILM. Because I figured I had nothing to lose I wasn't that nervous about the actual interview, which helped me answer their questions well. As luck would have it, they liked my portfolio because they were trying to get their first animated feature going. I knew things were getting serious when they started asking about my availability and salary.

I moved up north to work on the digital feature. Although the project never got made, I got to work with some of the most amazing artists like Iain McCaig, Erik Tiemens, Ryan Church, and Bill Perkins, to name a few. The first year on the job I made lifelong friends, rubbed elbows with people I had only read about in books, and probably learned more than I had in three years of art school.

My first feature-film credit came on Steven Spielberg's A.I. What an amazing project that was. Everyone in the entire facility was excited to work on it and it was a real pleasure. After a couple more years there, in 2002 I took a position as Art Director. Since then I've learned that time passes not in years but in projects, or, as we call them, "shows."

Even the best job might not be enough to satiate every appetite. After nine or ten hours at an amazing job like ILM, I can't wait to get home to create my own stories and worlds.

In the end there is nothing like creating your own ideas and being your own creative boss. Thanks to a very understanding and patient wife, the pages hereafter are what I do when I get home. Some of them are from stories inspired by poems or fairy tales, and some are just images that I think look interesting. One day I hope to write all of these stories down, but until then I hope these images will speak louder than words.

Thank you for picking up this book. I hope you enjoy my Tales.

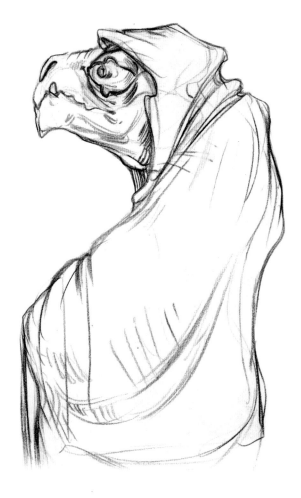

CHAPTER 1
SKETCHES

Many of the drawings in this book are from sketchbooks or the stacks of Post-it Notes I always have by my desk. the following drawings may not necessarily pertain to a finished painting, but can be thoughts or ideas, shape and pose tests or simply exercises to limber up my hand. Because sometimes its just fun to draw and see what happens. It's always the quickest way for me to see if my ideas will work, or if I even find them visually interesting.

For me, it's not about the specific type of pencil or pen. I'm more interested in the making of marks that have contrast or color. But for those of you who are curious about the technical, the following drawings were made from an array of pencils like Tombow, Papermate Sharpwriters or Prismacolors.

I've always believed that drawing is the most important skill for an artist to develop, as it is the foundation for other fine arts, such as sculpting or painting. I've discovered if I can't make a simple pencil-on-paper drawing work, then all of the Photoshop finesse in the world probably won't make a solid interesting image. If I have one piece of advice it is to draw often and draw fearlessly.

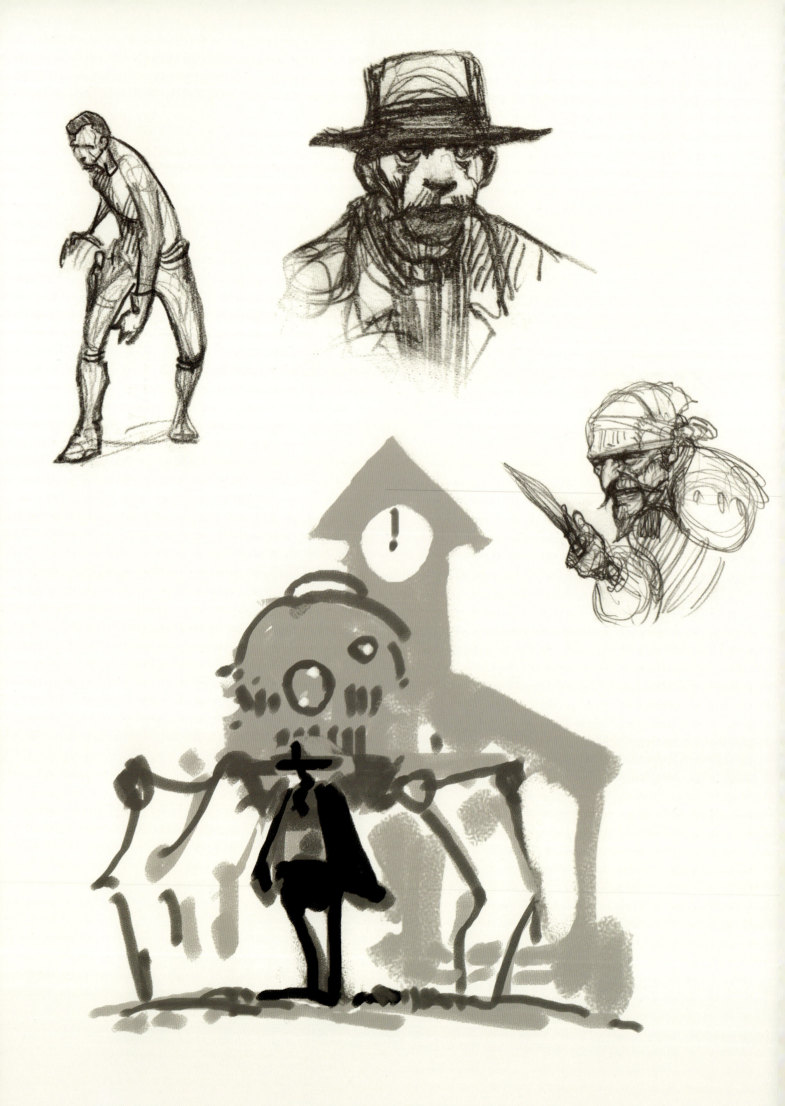

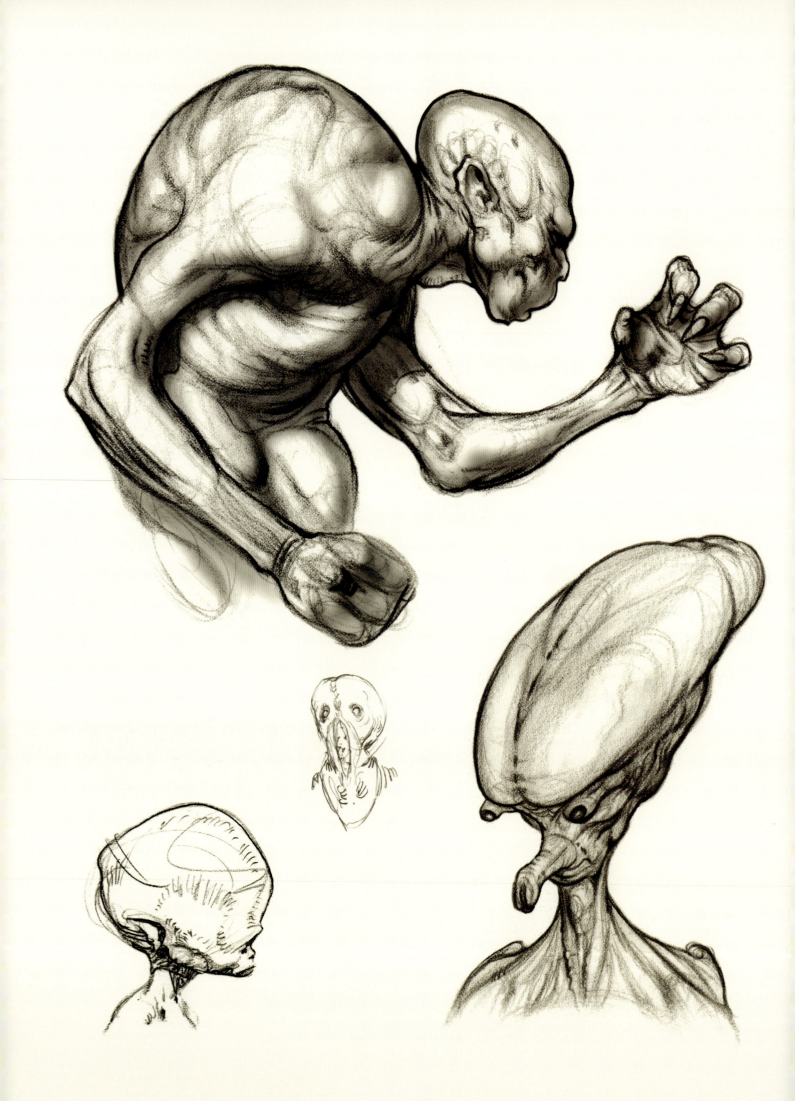

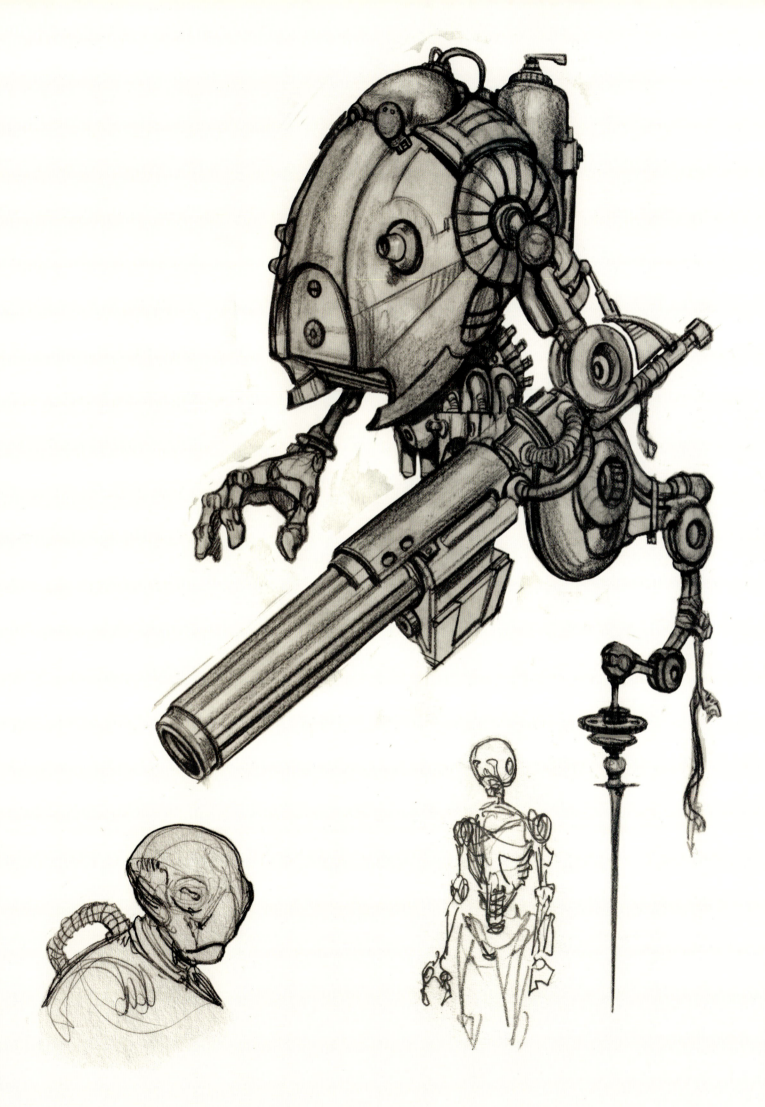

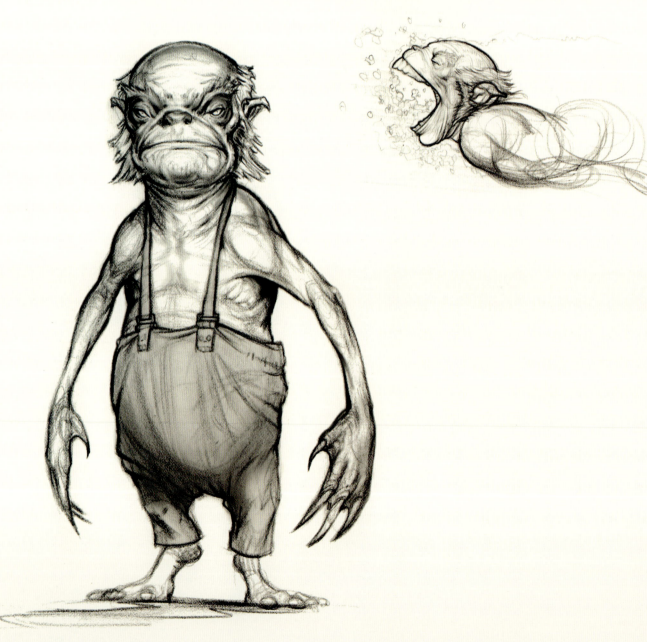

CHAPTER II
PAINTINGS

THERE ONCE WAS A KING WITH ONE DAUGHTER

There once was a king with a daughter so beautiful that she caught the eye of the lord of the dark fairies.

CRUSTS OF BREAD

A sister and brother are lured into a mysterious world from which there may be no escape.

Captain Gibbet

When captured, a pirate captain's punishment would often extend beyond death. Their bodies were enclosed in iron cages called gibbets and left to swing in the air until the flesh rotted off them. The bodies of captains such as William Kidd, Charles Vane, William Fly, and Jack Rackham were all treated this way.

Maintenance

In the hopes of maintaining his relevance, an aging human/robot hybrid oils his tarnished shell.

SLEEPING KINGS

A noble warrior's shortened life's story is inscribed on his crypt. A story repeated throughout history.

LISTENING (OPPOSITE)

A man lost in his grief over the death of his brothers ignores the living world around him.

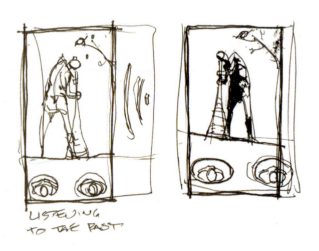

LEVEL SEVEN

Even evil creatures have to sleep. And if they sleep, they eventually must wake up.

LATE SPRING (OPPOSITE)

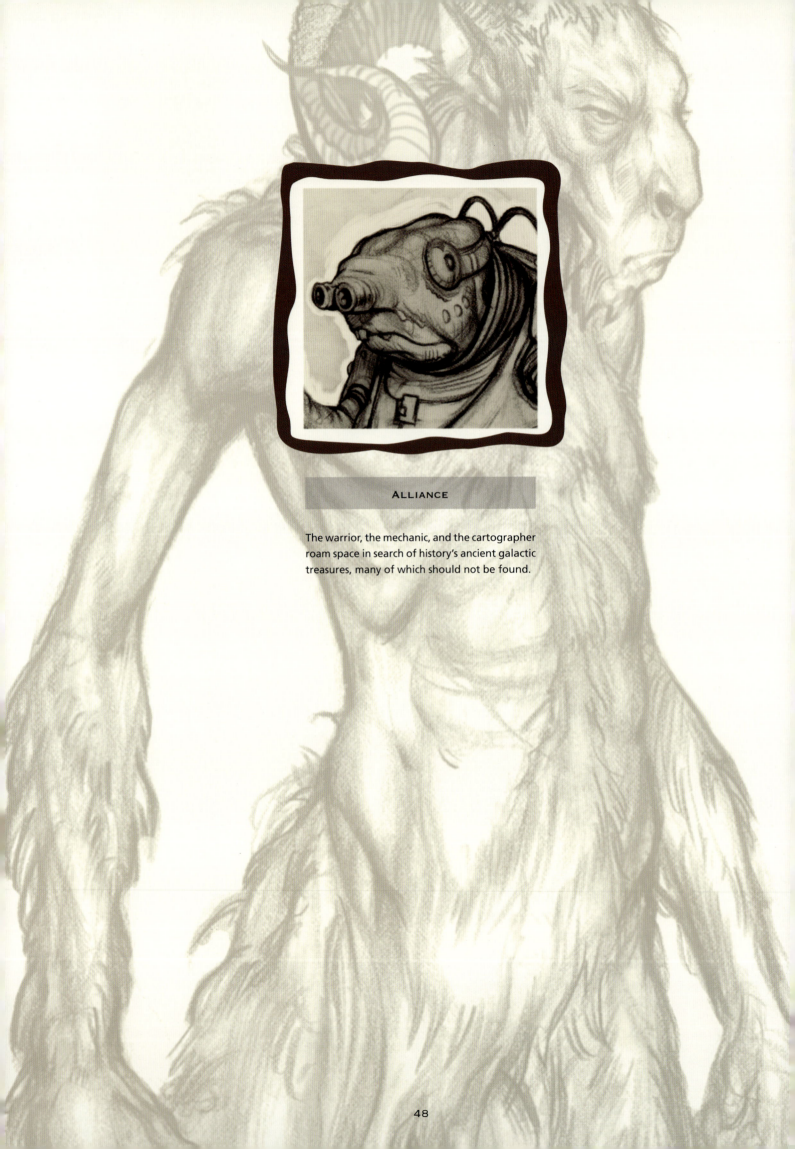

Alliance

The warrior, the mechanic, and the cartographer roam space in search of history's ancient galactic treasures, many of which should not be found.

THE JUNKYARD DOG

The reclusive owner of Jake's Junkyard fixes anything he can get his hands on. One night, he discovers an artifact most would have considered broken beyond repair. Now, Jake's new Junkyard Dog keeps watch over his precious yard and protects it from the robots that pilfer it.

| LAB RAT | What if Gulliver's Travels took place in the 1940s? |

| LOST CITY | Inspired by the movies I watched growing up, like Planet of the Apes. |

THE OTHER END — One wrong turn during a spelunking outing lands them in a new world.

EYE TO EYE — "It was the oddest thing to see those two faces, the golden face and the dead white face, so close together." Inspired by CS Lewis's The Lion, the Witch, and the Wardrobe

RAGE UPON HIM

"Scarcely had his hideous laugh rung out but once, when I was upon him."
A Princess of Mars by Edgar Rice Burroughs

BREACH

"He'd gotten used to the trick of perspective where it was never the ocean bottom going down, but always the vertical walls of water on either side growing taller." Olympos by Dan Simmons

BEGUILED

Many visitors to the forest have described strange lights in the distance. They are inexplicably drawn to them, and many are never heard from again.

THE NAMED SERIES

Author Claire Bell

Ratha, a member of a prehistoric sentient clan of wild cats, learns to tame a power that could upend worlds.

RATHA'S CREATURE

CLANGROUND

RATHA'S CHALLENGE

RATHA'S COURAGE

Darkwing

Author Kenneth Oppel.

"Air flowed around Dusk's sails and filled them. His shoulders and head lifted as he came out of his nosedive. He breathed in little gulps."

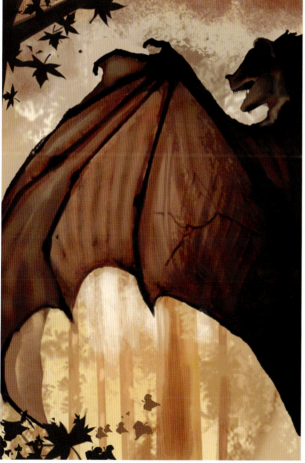

Preliminary Comps

Aftermath

The same mistakes are carried out over and over throughout time and on countless worlds.

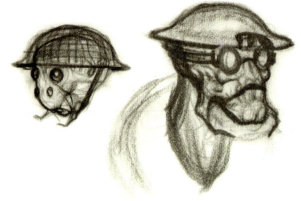

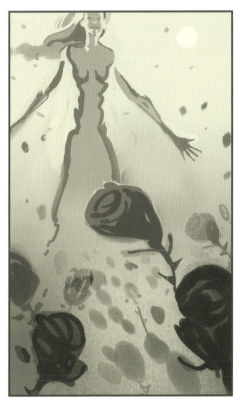

Ashley

She is coming of age and running free in a dangerous world.

BOND

Marooned without human contact and with only an upgraded mining robot to take care of him, Max grew close to his protector in spite of their differences.

BIASED

Most people didn't understand their friendship. But Lucy, fearing nothing, found a friend in a beast that all others feared.

This piece is all about visual irony. The first read on this image is supposed to be "What is that mechanical monster doing to that vulnerable girl?" The second read tells us that they're merely friends at play.

THE BOGEYPOOL

Accidents draw them close, and "accidents" keeps them. Whether in search of a lost ball or a lost pet they always find their way to her water's edge.

FRAZETTA TRIBUTE

This was a cover for the September 2007 issue of ImagineFX magazine. They wanted a Frazetta tribute cover that was also a tutorial. I love Frazetta but I also wanted to have my own spin on the image. I grew up loving Saturday morning cartoons, and one of my all-time favorites was Thundarr the Barbarian. So I skewed this Frazetta-style barbarian image in that direction.

TEAM TEST TUBE

Dahlia is a talented and frustrated animal-rights activist. Along with a big heart, she has a certain set of skills that make her unique to her world. Using those skills, she has freed a few test subjects, two of which are Chimp and Ed.

Chimp, who has had the brain of a scientist transplanted inside of him, is the genius of the operation. He always keeps his cool. Well, almost always. Ed was a super-soldier experiment gone wrong, or had it? Many of his powers are still unknown. Fueled by his favorite corn chips, he's the brawn of the group.

Together they use their combined skills to take down evil scientists and their labs.

FOREST WHISPER

While the tree and the wind play, the tree spirit can be seen near the tree she protects.

This piece was for an art auction to help save the Sayama Forest, the same forest that inspired the movie Totoro.

STORM BRINGER — A natural-disaster machine.

OFF TO BATTLE

One day soon, all of our wars might be fought with mechanical armies. What if World War II had been fought this way?

78

WRITHEA — Character study of a cold and soulless robot Medusa.

It Fled at the Touch

Day after day, Narcissus stared at the water, in love with his own reflection. He began to waste away from grief, until one sad morning he felt himself dying.

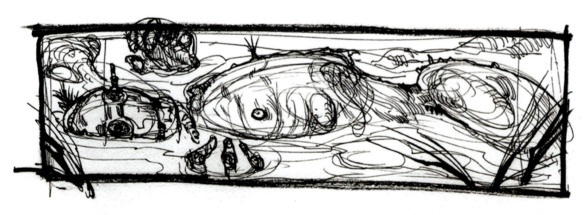

THE HILLOCK

The casual traveler of the forest never knows the histories upon which they tread.

FALL OF THE GLUTTON

Even in the underworld, the laws of nature are at work. The smaller demons work in packs to take down the larger ones.

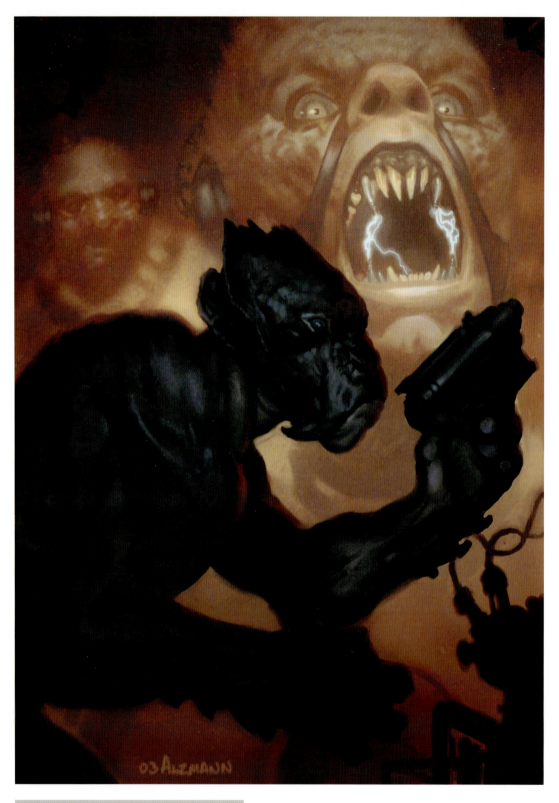

HUNTED

I took two genres that I love, film noir and sci-fi aliens, and merged them.

GATHERING — Nature is brutal, and everything has to eat something.

DRAW

Cowboys and robots: a perfect combination. Why not put two things you love together and see if there is a story there? I worked with steampunk designs for the robot, but in the end I thought a menacing 1950s-style robot would be a bit more original and more fun. I did this one for an instructional DVD for Gnomon. A couple of years later, as fate would have it, I worked on a film that had a similar setup.

Evolution

Destruction and creation are partners.

STATIONED

I painted this image after signing my first contract. At this point in my career, I didn't know if I was going to stay in one place and grow roots or move around from job to job.

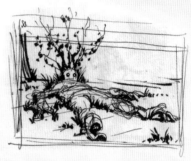

CHAPTER III

TUTORIAL

1/ Sketches

The concept of this piece is a group of Viking warriors going off to hunt a prize that would win them fame and glory. I started out sketching an array of warriors and their quarry. At this early point I'm looking to inspire myself so I can be excited about the next stages.

2/ Thumbnails

Now, I'm starting to think about composition. I started by drawing the elements that I knew I wanted. Since the whole piece was done in Photoshop, I can lasso those elements, move them around, scale them, and flip them as needed until I find the right composition.

3/ Choosing a Thumbnail

I've chosen a thumbnail that will tell the story and looks fun for me to paint. Now I focus on composition and poses.

I may draw up to 20 different poses in order to find my final choice.

4/ Blocking in Values

I start by blocking in the values in black and white while I refine the drawing right on top of the scaled-up thumbnail.

Sometimes I'll get really far with a painting just in black and white, and then add the color later. Black and white values are far more important than color.

5/ Color Blocking

The next step is dropping in some local color and getting an idea for the overall shapes and silhouettes. The most important colors you can put down at this point are the colors in the sky. Think about the time of day and the direction of the sun. The big environment colors like the sky and the ground color will end up mixed into everything in the scene.

6/ Local Colors and Layer Planning

I lasso each element off of the background so that the mountains, archer, buzzards, and ax wielder are on separate layers. The goal of this is to make painting up those elements easier.

I also use a color layer to give every item and material in the painting its proper local color.

7/ Second Pass to Stay Happy

Whatever you settle on will determine how good the piece is. If there is any little thing bothering you when you're working on a painting or drawing it won't go away. With time, it will only annoy you more.

In this case, everything in the composition felt too flat on the camera, so I re-drew the giant's head at more of a 3/4 angle.

I also decided to give the main warrior some horns on his helmet.

8/ Refining & Adjustments Layers

I add more color and paint to the giant and give his form more heft.

The warrior needed a stronger feeling of sunlight on him, so I used a levels adjustment layer to create a shadow side for him. By painting with white and black in the mask of the adjustment layer, you can add or take away shadow.

9/ Painting & Refining

Now I can start painting opaquely. I refine the details as a whole as much as possible without focusing too much in one area for too long. Doing that will remove any "painterly" quality to the piece.

I add some sunken arrows in the giant's head and some blood-spattered snow beneath to add a bit of grit.

10/ Painting in Some History

I refine the warriors and add a light side to the face of the giant.

I also add more evidence of a battle and some caked-on ice and snow, basically trying to recreate the crime scene and give evidence that the warriors tried to move or drag the head a bit. I try to put history into every painting, drawing, and design.

11/ More & More Refining

Everything is coming more into focus. I add some highlights and some reflected light on the giant to make him look wet and add some detail in the background mountains.

12/ Little Changes Here & There

I brighten up the image with some more sunlight using a levels adjustment layer and a screen layer.

As the painting comes along I'll find new things that bother me, or I'll figure out improvements. Details will constantly change to keep me happy, such as the head of the ax, and wardrobe, such as the neck warmer on the archer.

13/ Testing a new Image Crop

I change the arm and hands of the main warrior and finally remove the wind from his cloak. It would have to be one heck of a wind to blow that heavy fur around. I give the giant more of a cast shadow and continue to refine the archer.

The biggest change here is the black bar on the right side of the frame. I often paint with a full black frame around my painting. By adding this black bar on the right as a layer I can contemplate cropping the image without having to commit to it.

14/ Adjustment Layers to Finish

I beef up the ax and flip the buzzards so that they are flying into the composition. I warmed up the entire piece and added some more details in the background clouds.

Often at the end of a painting, I might add a color-balance adjustment layer over the top to unify the colors. This is very similar to glazing a transparent color over the top in oils. I'll crop the piece now and use any other adjustment layers to add depth or contrast.

Afterword

by Iain McCaig

I have just watched Christian Alzmann create a concept design that will likely become an icon for an entire generation. He did it without breaking a sweat, or shirking his daily duties as Art Director on another project. He created several other images that day too, every one a winner. And he did it without staying up all night and missing the opportunity to have dinner with his beautiful wife. I suspect he slips out at night and fights crime, too.

When I first knew Christian, he was just a kid. He came to my home studio in San Anselmo to show me his portfolio, and I apparently told him to go to Art School and get some training. I can only assume that he listened, or was bit by a radioactive spider. By the time I saw him again, his art skills had jumped into hyperspace.

It's our job as artists to conjure illusions. People might imagine they come out of nowhere—straight out of our dreams, channeled from the collective unconscious, the product of talent or supernatural beings. Which of course is true. What is also true is that imaginations are not illusions but immanently practical things. Like giant melting pots, they extract and alloy ideas from the slag of observation. The fire that heats the pot, though, is the life of the artist itself. It goes without saying that a life well lived burns hotter than one that is shallow. The resulting art reaches beyond 'cool', not because it is any better drawn or designed, but because it is no longer illusion. The artist has created something real.

Such artists usually have those who seek to imitate them (a perfectly healthy practice, as long as you grow out of it). For those who would seek to imitate Christian and aspire to his kick-ass lighting, character design, and visual storytelling, remember you must also copy his sense of wonder, his contagious chuckle, and his kind and generous heart, for these are the things that give life to his images.

As for his frequent workout of running up and down the three hundred-odd Lyon Street steps…seven times …well, that just ain't human.

SPECIAL THANKS

To my parents: Walter and Anne Alzmann, and my Aunt Jeanne and Uncle Andy.

My childhood friends who liked my work in the earliest of years: John Darakjian, Elliot Mercer and Mark Williams.

To my mentors and teachers: Bob Kato, David Nakabayashi, Timothy Barnes, and Gary Meyer.

My peers and colleagues through the school years: Martijn Heilig, McNevin Hayes, Emily Caisip, Andy Lee, Jang Chol Lee, Kevin Chen, and Duke Beardsley.

My art support and the people who inspire me everyday at work: Aaron McBride, Robert Mackenzie, Carlos Huante, Iain McCaig, Susan Davis, Kelly Smith, Bill Perkins, and Craig Elliott

To George Lucas and Ralph McQuarrie for creating the first worlds that inspired me to draw.

To Scott Robertson, Tinti Dey, and Cecilia Zo at Design Studio Press for publishing this book and Anne Fisher Gonzales for her creative guidance.

Last but not least to Aaron McBride. Iain McCaig, Dylan Cole, Shelly Wan, and Dan Dos Santos for their kind words.